In memory
of
Sabrina Duffy

1987 - 2003

UNCHARTED

VOYAGE

Poems by students from Loreto Abbey Dalkey
Edited by Anne Fitzgerald

First published in 2004
by Loreto Abbey Dalkey Press
Loreto Abbey Dalkey
Co. Dublin
Ireland

Cover photograph © Anne Fitzgerald 2004

Printed and bound in Ireland by Wicklow Press Ltd.,
The Murrough, Wicklow

A CIP catalogue record for this book
is available from the British Library

ISBN 0-9547366-0-5

Introduction

All of us have the gift of poetry – to a greater or lesser extent. The ability to view the world through a poet's eye is an intrinsic part of childhood. Patrick Kavanagh wrote of "the newness that was in every stale thing/ When we looked at it as children". In order to retain this precious gift and to explore it fully, we must journey deep within ourselves.

The title of this volume of poems is Uncharted Voyage. It contains the work of pupils from the Transition Year, who have travelled inward in search of words and rhythms which express their vision of the world and in some cases which articulate very personal thoughts and emotions. Often it is in the act of writing that we discover our deepest feelings, which are then borne to the surface by means of words. Through language the experience of living is thus transfigured into the art of poetry.

Like all arts, poetry has an element of craft, which must be learned. What better teacher than a person who is herself a practitioner of the art. The contributors to this book were fortunate in having Anne Fitzgerald, a past pupil of our school, as their mentor. Under her guidance they gained insights into the making of poems.

When we read a poem it can appear as if it just flowed from the writer's pen with little effort. Even the greatest poets, however, think deeply about their work, shaping and reshaping the words until they sound as if they have evolved naturally. W.B. Yeats had this in mind when he wrote "A line will take us hours maybe;/ Yet if it does not seem a moment's thought,/ Our stitching and unstitching has been naught."

All the contributors to this book deserve our thanks and our congratulations for the work they have produced. We are particularly grateful to Anne Fitzgerald, not only for the tremendous interest she has taken in the project, but for her generous gift of a poem, which we are delighted to include in what we hope will be the first of many publications by our students.

Dolores MacKenna
Principal,
Loreto Abbey, Dalkey

1

Contents

4

8

Sarah Byrne

Whiteness

I stand out in the cold
one winter morning,
gaze up at the sky,

watch snow fall
around me and stick
to the ground nearby.

Winter

Winter is so special
in many ways.
It brings longer evenings
and shorter days.

Grainne Delaney

Watching Summer

When the sky is blue and cloudless
everyone goes to the beach.

The sea draws attention to the world
about me; sun glistens off blue.

I see three angels walk in front of me
carrying gold crosses close to their hearts.

Blue gowns with white wings open clouds —

Iréine Dorgan

On the Bridge

With my whole life before me
on this side of the bridge
my adventures are busy here
but the far side looks calmer

and invites me. I take my first step,
crystallised earth crunches beneath
my feet, my breath fades into air.
In the middle opportunity stands

as if a mountain. I close my eyes
and when I open them I will have walked
and walked until I have reached
spring on the other side.

New Angel

It has been a long hard year
which you fought with a smile.

You never gave up, always pushing
yourself that extra mile.

No words can describe
the inspiration you gave.

Now, you are through those gates
being minded by Kings.

Alison Dunne

The Abandoned Bicycle

Blue skies all about,
bright sun shining down,

shimmering seas beside me,
golden sands beneath my feet,

the day I found a bicycle
left at my front door.

It was old and grey
and the colour of hay.

Christmas Eve

On Christmas Eve night
I woke to a fright
to hear Santa's sleigh
land on our roof.

I jumped out of bed,
ran down the stair
to see Santa at our tree
leaving presents for me.

I went back to bed,
and covered my head,
woke in the morning
to see what was left for me.

Annie Tobin-Dunne

Grace Notes

When I close my eyes,
music plays its sad song.

I think of you and smile
cherishing our memories
falling like a perfect octave.

Shauna Doyle

Love

I hate the cold, wet weather,
the darkness in night
and my dullness of days.

I hate the lessons we must learn
in life to help us reach the person
we will become.

I hate the judgment and the fear
but mostly I hate the fact
that you are not here.

Daydreaming

It is a sunny afternoon
when life takes me by the hand
to skip through woods.

I sing songs of far-off lands
beneath a starry sky
until day is, no more.

I am peaceful as a cloud
so far away from cities.
I linger in the air, heaven bound.

Tara Flood

Leaving

Sad and alone in this darkened place
with nothing to lighten my life,
I feel torn from the world,
no one to comfort or protect me.

After walking through that door
there is no turning back.
I have to make my own way.
Yet, could that light ahead

be welcoming me, showing the way?
Alone, yet this light above comforts
and protects me like a friend
helping me to find my place.

Forever Longing

Searching through the older me
I wonder; will I have a chance
to find my better self,
or to watch the sun set orange
before it sails for the horizon.

Gemma Foley

In the Desert

My soul is as lonely as a man
roaming the desert.

My heart yearns for love as a man
in the desert yearns for water.

I look around for a friendly face as a man
in the desert looks for cacti.

But I, like him, can only see things
that are not truly what they seem.

The Boy

As I look across the room
our eyes meet.

You stole my heart
as our eyes met.

Katie Galvin

Wintering White Water

And like a blanket you cover the world.
It is time for dark evenings, fires in hearths and family.

Outside snowflakes float silently to ground
as my father drags a green tree through the door,

we cheer, *Christmas is coming, Santa is on the way!*
Decorations hang on every branch, presents are placed

beneath, for the big day. When it comes, all the world
looks white and anticipation is unwrapped.

Down to Earth

I am a cloud, floating up high
watching the world go by.
I see laughing people cry.
Sometimes I see nobody at all.

I am a cloud, who works in an office
sitting at a desk. I swing around
and around, on my office chair.

I am a cloud, who walks the city
along concrete paths
crashing into brick walls.

Sarah Kate Geraghty

Looking for Logic

Why has everything got a point
and everything is always neat
in rooms that are usually square?

Sometimes people are on the brink
of spiralling out of control, round
and around, circling circles,

going nowhere, unlike rain.
Soaked to the skin, people stand
out clearly, seen for what

they are for the first time.
Where do the fairy people of myth
and legends go; where do we go?

Changes

Autumn is old meeting new.
Fallen leaves orange, silver clouds rise
as the wind blows stronger.
Flower beds disappear
and the world looks different.

Sarah Louise Hassett

In Full Effect

Sometimes we feel trapped inside the body
of our lives. Everything can be so difficult.
Some do so much they feel overwhelmed
by work; others are lonely doing so little.

It is all about choices. Red is the centre of it all;
different squares come from different centres.
Lots conform to rules and become a new shade.
Then there are those who think outside the box

considered dull and put behind the squares.
Around the edges it is rough and mixed up
as left out shirts of civilisation. Inside you see
clearly each idea with its different meaning:

blue is for power, yellow for loneliness,
red is for revenge and green is jealously.
But then again hidden under all colour
is that mellow human nature.

Two Seasons

1
As I run through freshly fallen leaves
they crunch beneath my feet.
I feel comfort in their orange-yellow.
It is the time of the year we light fires;
red flames flicker and burn our way.

2
Last Friday my friends and I frolicked
through lovely fields.
We soaked up the yellow sun;
such golden pleasure rays we got.

Then the heavens opened, pouring down
on us in our belly-tops and shorts.
We laughed and cried and got the flu.

Roisin Hearns

I Love Winter

everything is dark with bright lights.

When the days start getting shorter
you know you will get less sleep
but it will be nice.

Every house will have its fire lit
when it is wet and raining outside
but inside it is nice and warm.

When you go out you wrap up
warm with hats and gloves.
Things stay cold and refreshing

when you are out having fun.
And when Christmas comes everyone
seems to be in a better mood.

Here and There

In this white room it seems cold and bare
a door leading to the outside looks bright.

Though this room is dull and bare it may be
safer with just you and your thoughts,

safer than in the outside world with all its hurt
and pain. The bareness here allows you to dream.

Claire Horgan

What Do You See

A strange looking woman with her family
or a beggar in rags with a plea in her eyes.
She asks for money from passers-by.

A scary old witch with a frightened face
with wrinkles and bags all over the place
or a loving mother who is trying so hard
to give her children the life she never had.

On a Beach

We lie on this beach, listen to the waves
breaking quietly, lapping gently against
the pale yellow sand.

The fresh air —
sparkling water,
reflecting the sun's golden rays.

The children are laughing once again
playing like they used to.
We have no worries here, surrounded

by turquoise skies and golden beaches,
for the past is behind us and things
we have yet to find are in our futures.

Rachel Howard

Three Months Off

No more school
Horray! Horray!
School is out for the Summer.

The sun beams down,
it gets very hot.
Children play on streets
till darkness comes.

The airports are packed,
the traffic is bad.
Parents are cursing and ask
When do these children go back?

Measurement

Time is one of the most important objects in life.
You could not depend on the brightness of the light.
If it was dark tonight would you guess it was twelve?
You would need a clock to help you out.

In order to work you need time, an hour to be in.
Otherwise how can one know when one is due?
So, get a watch on your wrist and you will never be late again.

Katie Kelleher

Questions

A man watches as cars go by.
He wonders *why?*

Why is the sky blue and the sun yellow,
why is the grass green? And when he wakes

in the morning he finds it hard to open his eyes.
Why is the world made up of these colours?

One Moment

The rush of cold up your back
is like a thousand daggers gently
piercing your skin

and the breath pouring out
of your mouth
like steam from a kettle.

The dampness in the air feels so cold
that it would freeze you, preserve
your milky skin, so fragile and so sensitive.

Ornaith Killen

That Nervous Feeling

Watching people who are waiting
makes you want to giggle.
Looking at their expressionless faces
and listening to their exasperated sighs,
seeing their faces slowly change
from that blank look to being nervous
the closer their appointment looms.

And you flood with relief
as it slowly dawns on you
that they are showing exactly
the same symptoms that you are feeling.

Spring

Ring those bells.
Shout down wells.
This is done to show
that Spring has sprung.

Shoots on trees,
hear those bees,
and the trickle of
fresh water being tickled.

Ailbhe O'Higgins

Credo

I believe in courage
in trying new things
and achieving our goals.

I believe we all
have our strengths
and equal opportunities.

I believe in never being scared
and that we should always
follow our own dreams.

In the Beginning

Colours are bright,
I can see them so clearly:
reds, yellows and blues.

When they begin to fade,
they go further and further away.
Now they are not so clear

the objects are smaller
and covered by mist.
Gone into the distance for no one to see.

Holly Ovington

A Safe Place

It makes me feel alive
and at the same time strangely humble.
Compared to it I am nothing.
I am invisible, but not forgotten.

If only I could stay here
and appreciate this wonder,
hidden by such greatness.

I feel more alive
and stronger than I have ever been.
I hope that if it should go
this new me would not vanish with it.

Below

Too far under,
too deep to make it through
too far beneath the surface
too deep to call to you.

So far from everyone
pretending to be well
pretending to be happy
hoping I can tell.

Yet, despite your front
you hope I can save you.

Emer Ryan

Isolation

I am all alone,
unable to talk to anyone.
I feel different and
on my own against the world.

I look around and see
no happiness, just a dull landscape
inside where I hide.

So, when I look from the inside-out,
see people having fun, I know I am
not ready to join their outside world.

Whisper

Little
children
kick
fallen leaves
on their way
to school,
walking
through
the park
where
squirrels
hide
their food.

Sophie Shanley

Covered Up

In the brisling heat of the desert
a lone man walks on scorched sand.
He wears a blue gown to match his sky
and is slowing down in such heat.

I watch and want to help him
so, I make myself visible.
He makes his way towards me
with such masculine grace.

We are standing face to face,
I am in awe at his beautiful eyes.
From his dark lashes and almond
shaped lids, a smile breaks through.

November

Everyone wraps up
hats and heavy coats come out.

Car windows frost over
grass crunches beneath your feet.

Children put away
their Hallowe'en costumes

and begin their Christmas lists.
Fires are lit and rooms light up.

Rebecca Sheehy

Wind

Evergreens stand tall and still;
others are bare with little
or no leaves to cover their bodies.

Cold wind moves through the air
even though things remain stiff;
it swirls over snow-covered

mountains and tree-tops,
and brings with it
the movement of Winter.

Sea of Sorrow

Drowning forever in her sea of sorrow
she carries her hurt and pain
inside her frozen heart.

She looks up at the falling rain
falling deeper and deeper into her past.
Pain crawls through her veins

filling her soul with sadness
for the present. Mistakes flood her mind
dragging her down and down.

Niamh Whelan

Our Tree

When days get shorter
and the nights are longer,
when it is wet and windy,
it means Christmas it coming.

Green and red decorations
go up in our house.
We put lots of lights on our tree
and sit an angel on top.

When our house needs to be heated
we light a fire to warm us up
while we wait for Christmas to arrive.

White Man

I build a snowman and wonder
will he still be standing in the morning?

I wake to a bright sunny day;
my snowman has melted away.

Fiona Byrne

Broken Promises

When I was small
and cut my knee
you fixed me up
and took care of me.
I was your baby
you'd stop my crying.
I knew you'd be there
time after time.

As I grew older
the love stayed strong.
In my times of doubt
you were never wrong.
I am still your baby.
You'll never stop trying
time after time.

When I got married
and had kids of my own
you were by my side.
I was your baby
even though I have mine.
You will be there
time after time.

Now you have gone
I can see you no more.
You cannot stop my crying
as you did before.
You said you'd be
there time after time.
I believed you
but you were lying.

Sarah Carroll

Night

Close your eyes my love:
Sleep through time
in your warm bed,
dream of fluffy clouds,
let the thunder become music,
hoping you will awake to a new day.

West of West

A cowboy
in the sunset
— a lone stranger

A cowboy
on the range
— a horseman

A cowboy
in a house
— our father

A cowboy
in my memory
— a lover.

Aoife Corrigan

You

You come to me
dream-like, the kind
that always leaves
just as the best part starts.
It ends so abruptly
not unlike growing up.

Alice Cryan

Damp Dark Caves

The light shines through
dark damp caves.

The river flows through
dark damp caves.

Birds fly into
dark damp caves.

Insects crawl up
dark damp caves.

Infants are born inside
dark damp caves.

Life breaths inside
dark damp caves

until the caves are damp
and dark no more;

but full of day's life
until night, when once

again damp dark caves
will reunite.

Andrea Doyle

Daisy

We lay her down beside a cross
her snow-white coat against the dark soil
curled up as if she were sleeping by the fire.

Her unused eyes were closed;
they had caused her death.

I looked up, other mourners gathered:
Toby, Cloudy and Snowy, to say
goodbye to our much loved friend.

The Fugitive

A seventy-year old man listens to a radio
...*Sunny spells and scattered showers...*
Outside dogs howl for their breakfast
loud crackles echo from the market below.

And as he puts a foot out the door
sweat pours down his face, afraid
he will be caught.

Deirdre Gill

Your Lake Spirit

This is my new special place if I look
hard enough I can almost see your face.
The sun reflecting on water reminds
me of how you use to paint this scene.

Your colours were always so exact
so bright like you, you used such a mix.
You loved this place saying, I could
die here, but never disappear.

Cityscape

Here in this city I feel
trapped and unwanted.

The roads are busy and loud.
The sky is grey and full of cloud.

I want peace and quiet
to be free from this racket and riot.

I want to be in the sunshine all day long
where I can be, finally completely free.

Edwina Grehan

Journey

I am sitting on the Dart thinking about stuff.
People are talking but I cannot hear a sound.

I stare out the window watching everything go by
I feel so lost, I cannot even cry.

It is hard to explain how I feel, I do not know why
someone would not reach out and lend me a hand.

In every seat people sit
but I am the only one on my own.

So Cold

Your heart is like ice
you will not let me in.

Your heart is like ice
you're as hard as a tin.

Your heart is like ice
small, grey and sharp.

Your heart is like ice
giving me no chance.

Kate Grehan

Feeling Trapped

Why do I feel trapped when all around
me the colours of beauty and freedom
fill this city, as if sounds of laughter.

Alone in this room, no one hears my cry.
The world is too busy to look up at the sky.

Is the sun laughing at me, are birds
mocking my call? Clouds tease me

with their freedom and the sky
does not care at all.

Will anyone rescue me,
might a gold-hearted knight?

No one knows I am here, having turned
their backs on me, and grown cold.

Uncharted Voyage

I wonder what the sea has seen
on its journeys through the years.

Perhaps a pirate battle roared long ago,
men with eye-patches and parrots at their ears.

Cannons roaring, swords flashing
and stolen gold hidden in timber cracks.

The sea holds sinking ships and dying people.

Mary Clare Healy

Swinging

Up I go
it is a wonderful sight.
To and fro
my heart fills with delight.

Forward and back
like a pendulum's beat.
I swing and sway
the world at my feet.

High in the sky
low in the grass.
I watch birds fly
I see worms pass.

If I had a wish
it would simply be,
to take this swing
to heaven with me.

God's Beams

At the tender age of eleven
two pearly beams came
downwards from heaven.

I gaze out my window
stare at the land, a magic
beauty covers the sand.

Ailbhe Heffernan

Stairway

Everyone must climb
one step at a time.

Each step is different
each brings its own surprise.

No matter, for upwards
is where destiny lies.

Some are spiral, others straight,
but it is what's up above

that keeps us climbing
up and up.

Ailbhe Kavanagh

The Birthday Shelf

There it sits
the ideal gift.

Two days to go
until I will lift

it up in my hands.
Perfectly wrapped

I place it back
the way I preferred.

Freedom

We have seen things
you would not dream
of, hurt and deceit.
Now we are free from
this miserable life.

White people came
to our homes, uprooted
us, forced us out
of the world we knew.

We have returned
to a different life.
Our families are gone
we are alone, scared
of this new freedom.

Jennifer Kenny Boyd

From Where I am Standing

I find a magnificent building and would die
for the chance to capture its image on camera.

Standing close to it, the paint is chipped
while the windows are far from genuine,

and like so many things in life it is not
as good as it seemed from a distance.

Life Guard

I sit perched on a high beach chair
drifting off to an unknown place.

I stare, trance-like into the blue horizon
drifting off to an unknown place.

I hear laughter. No. Shouting. I quickly
drift back to earth, having forgotten my place.

Fiona Kilfeather

Perspective

A tower rises
above distant hills
red-bricked houses
surround its base.

In the foreground
green leaves turn brown
reminding me of you.

You were tall and bright,
you were the tower rising
above the distant hills.

Suzanne Larrigan

7A Bus Route

As I sat gently down
on the soft seat
I let out a sigh of relief.

I looked out at the dark
day, wind was swirling,
snow falling to ground.

Slowly with the heat
on the bus, my rosy nose
started to tingle,

I could feel it again.
And then the 7A came to a halt
for me to face the cold of day.

Solo Sketch

With her thin face drawn weak
from being too much alone
her dark eyes are heavy with bags.
She walks round shouldered
carrying no pride.

Helen McGoohan

Spanish Waiter

I remember him standing there
thirty yeas before, holding a rose saying amour.

My Spanish Waiter, my holiday romance,
a pity I could not stay; we did not have a chance.

I took my flight home, feeling rather sad
but I am sure my husband Jimmy
would have been quite mad.

Tempus Fugit

A quiet day in the country spent with my Dad
and me, picking blackberries, watching passers-by.

We lounged in the tall grass and fished in the lake.
What a shame this was a chance we did not take.

If I had seen what would happen to the time we would lose,
a day in the country I would more often chose.

I couldn't have predicted that crack in the glass
the swerving and crashing through the grass.

Daddy, I screamed, scrambling out of the car
I bent over Daddy and listened to his heart

I could hear no thump-thump, or sound from his breath
I didn't know what to do, so I bent down and wept.

Anna McKeown

And There We Arrived

The boat's hull glided through clear water
reaching golden sand where we stepped out.

Hot sun kissed our skin as warm sand hugged
our feet and the water lay quiet.

From the wooden boat we gathered our possessions
to explore the silence and the breeze.

Where I Hide

No one can see me
but I can see them.

Behind the long grass,
I can see my village where
torture is happening.

The sea is my refuge
the grass my shield where
no one can see me.

Joanna Mullen

Room for Rent

They found her body on the ground
though still alive she made no sound
dying face down in a pool of sick.
The ambulance arrived quick, quick,
yet still too slow for the girl — so young.
The liver damage had begun
her organs failed, and though they tried
in the end she simply died.
A sixteen-year old girl — so young,
all she'd wanted was some fun.
So, she lied and stole a car
and rented a room above a bar.
She thought it was a place to hide.
Instead it was the place she died.

Flowers of Innocents

It looked so pretty, all white and sweet
a friendly face I came to meet.
Each day I'd walk right through that field
and at the very spot I'd yield
to gaze upon that glowing white
until of course, came that mighty unknowing.

Here was someone who couldn't care
for something so gentle and sweet,
someone who knocked me from my feet.
He hit me hard and stole my money.
Now I bleed where white flowers once stood
the spot lies drenched in my blood.

Aoife Nolan

Not for Tourists

By a calm lake,
elaborate architecture stood
above solid stone steps,
running across, a bridge,
arches and fancy pillars stand.

Windows are smashed and not replaced.
In a derelict building above the river
a girl hides under a rippled blanket, unnoticed.

Escaping

From my apartment you can view the city
with the eyes of a bird, see glittering lights
in houses below, like a Christmas tree at night.
I can almost forget about where I am
as I spread by wings and take flight.

Sarah Noone

Breaking through Clouds

I sit upon this hill today
and watch the sun break through clouds,
high above that little town
waiting for people to go about their day.

I sit upon this hill today
and watch the sun break through clouds.
I think about my family
and wonder, why they do not care for me.

I sit upon this hill today
and watch the sun break through clouds.
I wonder if I am really here —
why do people never notice me?

I sit upon this hill today
and watch the sun break through clouds —
I am starting to get bored up here
I think I will go back down.

Monday

With thick white snow on the ground
I could not hear a sound.

I looked at him as he stood there
his gorgeous jet black hair.

To see him was what I wished for, all day —
and just for a glance, I would even pay.

Claire O'Connor

Tragedy

All they wanted was some fun.
When they got into his car
they didn't know they'd go so far.

Going so fast, they couldn't scream
thinking it was just a dream,
swerving quickly into a tree.

There was nothing anyone
could do to save the car
or the teenage crew.

Seascape

Deep is the sea, high are its waves.
Bright is the sun up in the sky
casting shadows on the land
as frothy waves engulf the sand.

Seagulls soar overhead
while crabs dance on the seabed.
Fish flounder in the waves
and children play in caves.

Eiméar O'Connor

The List

My thoughts are running wild,
I don't know what to do.
I am picturing the worst case
and I am scared it might come true.

What will happen to me
if they find out what I do?
Nothing seems to be happening,
will it all fall through?

I am terrified of losing their trust
when they find out what I do.
I will be in a lot of trouble
please tell me what to do.

My Homestead

Going back to the place that was mine.
That place where my memory likes to shine
friends and acquaintances in every day
hustle and bustle in places I used play.

Now I see it not in my mind.
I realise time has not been kind:
boarded up windows, wooden doors
rotting, wallpaper falling on dusty floors.

I regret going back, before
returning, my memory was fine.
My heart slammed to the ground
at what happened to my place of youth.

Méabh O'Hare

Barbie Doll

With her yellow-white hair
and waist as thin as her neck,
she slips her crooked feet
into red shiny high heels.
Her blank blue painted eyes
issue a challenge, *come follow me.*

I lie in the narrow hospital bed
my bones jutting out unnaturally.
My eyes are dull and faded.
It is only now I realise,
I don't want to follow anymore,
but to find a way to stop.

Inside the Dome

Looking up
my neck is sore,
my eyes are drawn above:
Cherubs and angels on clouds
golden saints and ornate stars
watch creatures and devils
all swirling, making me dizzy
with the height of history.

A camera clicks
and I am back to earth
inside this church where tourists
photograph what I have seen.

Aoife O'Neill

Hailstones

It seems stupid how it can be so cold
and the sun shining like a summer's day.

Then white hailstones fall
crashing soreness against my hands.

Looking out the window, hailstones lie still
frozen to the spot where they first fell.

Lighthouse Keeper

When all is peaceful in the lighthouse
and everything is standing still,
I look out on the sea ahead
where all I see, is a wide open road.

There I can get into a car
and drive to anywhere in the world
but when I look at the horizon
I feel I might fall off its edge.

Where would I go?
but keep on going, till I reach
a different lighthouse. The one
waiting for me on the other side.

Alison Smith

Heritage

Every morning I walk by it.
It has an ancient and dirty face.
It gives the town an unwelcome look.

Some say it is the most historic landmark
in Connacht, but I wonder?
It is at its best when soft snow has fallen,

covering the past white.

On the Inside-Out

Old and haggard that is all you see.
Try to believe that, that's just not me.

Outside, I am sharp and mean
but inside I am not what I seem.

Clodagh Smith

Echo

Trapped, as cold as a stone
behind barbed wire
I long for home.

Here there is no escape.
No matter how loud I shout
there is no one to hear me.

One Little Window

This dark little room
is my favourite place.
Compared to outside,
there is not much space.

Within these four walls
I feel I am safe
with a little window
that does not stand tall.

Through my window the world
is too big and scary. No sound
of animals walking the ground
here, no movement, just stillness.

Siobhan Byrne

One for the Road

Why did they leave me?
I did not want them to go
leaving me with nobody.

Now they are together,
together they are away.

I need them here with me.
My parents are gone forever.

Someone should have told
that stranger not to drink and drive.

Inner Strength

When you feel everything
is upside-down, look beyond it.
You will see flowers and sunshine
and the hope of a brand new day.

Bora Cha

History Class

Have you ever thought
about that other country,

where they wear their customs
and bow down upon their knees?

Perhaps they are making sacrifices
to their own ancestry, in another place,

while we are studying in a school like this.

Taking a Rest

Why don't we take a rest
like one of the clouds in the sky
and think about our days past
like the salmon who migrate.

Elizabeth Drury O'Neill

Measuring Space

Time stands still,
clocks and watches stop.
Hands and numbers
will not move.

Hours turn into seconds,
seconds into hours,
everything is muddled.

Time is not a thing but a place
that is as endless and vast
as eternity itself.

Street Art

They want to get their hands
on something, anything,
that will take the paint.

But in the deep unknown
ice is overpowering,
and mother nature rules.

Kristina Earley

What Could Have Been

Looking back, I wonder
what would it have been like
to live in an old shanty town
and own an old bike?

I would have taken her out
and have shown her all the wonders
if they are still to be found.

And when I got home
I'd have shined her real nice,
before tucking her up for bed
in the green garden shed.

True Love

Are millions of people really in love
or is it just a state of mind?

And what of love at first sight
could it really exist?

Lia Glynn

Honest Work

Early morning sees us set
off for the golden field.

There we will save hay
late into the afternoon

until the hot sun grows
cool, in the blue sky

as we prepare
to stop.

Below the Arch

Above the bridge;
it is all hustle and bustle.

People rush from place to place,
cars race down streets.

Below the bridge,
only the sound of water

against the boat is heard,
guiding the river to the sea.

Julie Graham

Tradition

I sit on these rocks and think
about when we came here.

We would run and play
on summer's days.

When my children are born
I will bring them here

so that they might play and run
under the same sun.

Prayer for an Angel

I wish I could see her
I wish she was nearby.
I should have told her
what I really thought.
I knew from the start
she belonged to God.
I knew she knew
one day she'd depart.

Stephanie Lord

Steps

Who knows where they lead
or where I might end up?

Glancing back it is all so familiar
a multi-colour haze, ablaze.

I could sit down a while and rest
just for a short break.

All the Trappings

I don't know where I am, I'm lost.
It is cold and covered in frost.
I am scared, shaking, wanting warmth
I want to know I shall come to no harm.

I got myself into a mess,
wealth, fame and success.
What went wrong? I am not quite sure
but the place I am in has no cure.

Want, greed and ruthlessness
I am guilty of, I must confess.
Using any means I could
to get exactly what I wanted.

Laura Lynch

Snow

It doesn't happen often,
but when it does
who can complain.

The weather is just
at its worst. More than rain!
oh, what a pain.

When you look at it closely
and see the small grains
you will see their beauty

and you will gain the joy
that others share for these
small white little grains.

Karen McArdle

The Night before Christmas

Christmas Eve's a worrying night
hoping you won't wake up
and give Santa a fright.

You think you hear bells on top
of your roof. You're sure you can
hear the sound of Rudolph's hoof.

You are hoping he'll get
his pies and beer, and wonder how
he gets down the chimney each year.

You don't know how he does it
but frankly who cares? For maybe
next year he'll come down the stairs.

Sonja MacCurtain

Going Home

Houses, walls, streetlights
flash in the wink of my eye

as I sit on the train.
The air is hot and stuffy

making my nose runny.
I want to get home to rest

my bones on the couch
and watch some telly.

I had a hard day in the office,
annoyed my bosses

by making huge losses.
The train pulls into the station

I take a deep breath
and step into the rain.

Epiphany

We drive down a country road
in Dad's old Ford Escort.
Suddenly it give out a splutter
before coming to a stop.

Dad gets out to have a look
under the hood. I watch the rain,
and through the window
I see a beautiful carved face

staring back, her clothes shine
wet, statue-like. Dad gets in,
we drive away. I look back
watching her until she it out of sight.

Aoife Manahan

Family

Young children play
with toys on the floor
when unexpectedly
there is a knock at the door.
Their mother delivers
the news, it's your father...

In the funeral home
the long box brings tears
to their mother's eyes.
She is as white as a ghost.

In the church
the priest burns incense
as they walk by a sea of faces.

Back at their house,
family and friends mourn.
To this day the children
no longer play on the floor.

Gone

Good riddance to you, I thought, leave me alone
　I won't miss you, I won't be by the phone.
On Monday you were here spreading news
　of your wild journey. Who cares about my views?

Never thought I'd feel like this,
　very lonely with you to miss.
Every photo of you I feel I had to burn
　but now I'm endlessly awaiting your return.

Vanessa Murray

The Moon

is
a lollipop
against
a black sheet;
or
a light
for
when
it is
not bright.
It
blemishes
the
blackness
as a
nocturnal
boom.

Emma Naylor

Here I Am

Sometime ago I heard a man say,
If you want to make it, you
have to be powerful and big.

I thought nothing of it
until later that day.
I was stood on.

Can you see me?
I am the little green
thing in the corner.

Can you still not see me?
That is because you are
not looking hard enough.

Counsellor

She suggests I should go home
and look at the long ball of twine
that is my life.
                        Looking at it
I realise, there are many knots.
It is up to me to unravel them.

Lizzie O'Brien

Windows

Through openings
fresh air comes in,

past shutters: blue,
pink, and green

bringing colour
into the day.

Niamh O'Brien

Warning

I look around,
to my left and my right.
No one or nothing in sight.

I call into the distance,
my voice echoes —
nobody in the sea, but me.

Separation

It has been a long time since you went away.
Mum said you moved to a better place.

If that was so, I wonder why tears
were running down her face.

You left no warning, no note, nor call.
Sometimes I think she lied.

I miss your laugh and the games we played.
It is almost as if you died.

Amanda O'Connor

Celebrations

Family and friends are always there
when it matters; it is one
of the mysterious wonders of life.

They celebrate birthdays, christenings
and even Hallowe'en with you.
They are with you through the journey

so make the most of it, because nothing lasts.

Rosemary O'Connor

Betrayed

Why do you continue —
knowing our friendship
is tarnished?

It is hard to ignore
when trust
is lost.

Fiona O'Farrell

Sunset

Going down,
all over the bay
the big, bright sun
comes to say,
I'm all over the bay.
Darkness is falling
all over the town.
One, two, three,
it's down.

May Altar

She stands so delicate and tall
hoping that she'll never fall.

Mary has blue eyes and a blue veil.
Here's hoping that she'll never fail.

Flowers protect and make her bright.
She'll never let you run with fright.

Margaret O'Keeffe

In the Jungle

There appears to be a massive rumble
a gigantic feast for all sorts of beasts,
Oh! there must be ten million at least.

Monkeys, tigers and giraffes
and bears, bears; they are just
everywhere without a care.

Three women are coming bearing gifts.
Today all creatures join together; it fits
as all creatures unite with sheer delight.

My Grandfather

I sit here gazing at the bay
on this breezy autumn day

and I think of the hours
we spent together —

I know you will be
with me as I go through life.

Emer O'Leary

Watching Out for You

And as I sit here thinking of you
and of all the good times we had:

That time we sat in the park
watching leaves hustle under their trees.

Every Friday we'd go to the chipper
and sit on the bench outside.

When we went shopping we tried
on clothes, till we were thrown out.

The sun goes down beyond the horizon
as water gently ripples. I feel a light breeze

blowing across my face. I stand
to leave, thinking of you.

Hustle and Bustle

Horns beeping
babies crying
dogs bark,
bell towers chime
birds sing,
children playing.

Keri O'Neill

Picking Fruit

When I was smaller I recall
going blackberry picking
with my Dad and sister.
It was such an adventure
I'd put on my gloves to
ensure I'd not get pricked.

Aisling Redmond

Graffiti

Young and old join together
in different shades of blues, reds and greens.

All colours resemble each of us
with our little gifts of glory.

Graffiti writes words of colour
with symbols of love and hope.

Waves

Waves are rough and tough,
sometime they are dangerous.

Waves are fun to surf
and good to cool down
in the summer sun.

Karen Young

Buying Hope

The old shop on the corner
is no longer there.
Remember the days
we spent there, buying sweets
and hanging around.
When we got older
we bought bottles of cider,
which we could drink
till we hit the ground.

Ghosting

Snow falls heavy all night,
covering the castle in a blanket of white.

Morning comes and children play.
Night falls, they hope for another snowy day.

Clare Aughney

Interior

My house is damp and cold,
its walls are falling apart.

Isolated from everyone
it sits on top of a huge rock.

Up here I am on top of the world.
Below, sturdy colours of life

remind me of my happy childhood.

Invisible

I am not able to walk
or able to talk,

I am losing my sight.
Nothing seems right.

I am left all alone,
I try not to moan.

No one seems to care,
you have no time to spare.

You pass me by,
stare up at the sky.

Will nobody talk to me?
I may not be able to talk,

walk or see, yet I can
still hear you speak.

Hannah Brogan

The Heart of the Town

Church bells sound
at eleven-forty-five.

In a matter of seconds
empty streets are filled:

men, women and children,
young and old amble

arm-in arm over cobles,
talking of farming.

Inside, hymns and incense
help them take their seats.

Burnt to the Ground

As I look out over this marshland
I remember: the white window frames,
a little red door and the golden thatch
before fire ripped through it one night.

Emma Brown

Dublin Bay

Gulls diving and swooping
their hollow screeches fill the air.

The sea glistens pale yellow
in the last of evening light.

The sky is a kaleidoscope
of orange reds and pale blues.

I stoop to pick up
a handful of sand,

and feel its coarseness slip
through my fingertips.

Misunderstood

Huddled together,
we shelter from the storm —
together we'll stand tall.

People think us unjust
if we protect ourselves —
we'll carry on regardless.

We'll walk together
and hope one day
for acceptance.

Emma Flannery

Sailing

The steady tide of life
keeps me on course.
A row of caves looms ahead.
People watch, waving from above.

I glide aimlessly, uncertain of the way.
I am unsure and unafraid;
I will embrace whatever comes
with wide open arms.

Wind howls and I am shifted
into a faraway cave.
I don't emerge on the other side.
Black turns to white —

Drowning

One last gasp of breath
fills his every crevice.

He sinks as an anchor
moored to the ocean floor.

Jean Kelly

Beyond My World

In a land from the dawn of time
nothing else is real.

This city belongs to a broken dream
somewhere far off in the future.

Peace is here for life. God will shape
it with his hands of wind and sand.

Cunard Line

By the hall mirror leans a postcard of a ship.
It floats as if a cork upon the tide.
Seagulls fly about chimney smoke.
I travelled in uniform, worked for money
and was part of the dream.

Clare Kilty

The Harvesters

Women bend their backs,
arched like bridges
with folded knees.

Five fingers search,
finding the last sheaves.
They listen for fallen ears.

Men make towers
of mounting crops
piling them on wooden carts.

The sun is setting.
An empty field grows dark,
shadows are spreading —

Inversion

In the mist I see sand
half-drowned by tide.

It looks hacked and broken
as if attacked by a rusty nail.

The browning sand bleeds,
a victim of the tide.

Half-submerged in salty water
the cone looks like a sunken ship.

Ayano Iida

Letter to Santa

It's not bad
to go for a walk
on a lovely day.
It's just for contentment.

It's not easy to walk
in a snowstorm, but
these days things are
not so readily available.

Presents for me are
just sitting down and
watching through
the window.

Please Santa,
give me the energy
to walk in the
snowstorm.

Rachel Lundy

Tomorrow

I wish it could be better than today;
my worries might have gone away.
I would have no one to please.

Night Terror

Lost in solitude, nowhere to go
a heavy fog hangs low in the sky,
a certain eeriness lingers —
broken by a scream.

Running, panting, my heart
beats quicker; I am afraid to
look behind me.

I stop to rest, out of breath and
exhausted, I hear a wolf howl.
Strange images fill my mind —

Slowly I drift away, leaving
my thoughts behind. The weight
is lifted as I awake to the light.

Aoife McCambridge

Dreaming

Looking deep into painted mountains,
carries you along. Such a vast range
of emotions in each coloured stroke.

They say whatever you want,
wild artists strokes of unknowing,
but dreaming is the key.

Light bursts through
like an escape tunnel
calling to you.

Contrast

What a contrast there is
between the dark strong sea
and the pale gentle horizon.

What a contrast there is
between the gentle waves
and the black shadow-land.

What a contrast there is
between the distant background
and the forceful foreground.

What a contrast there is
between our ways of thinking —
the difference is you and me.

Niamh McCaughey

Vacant

Every morning he sits in the same seat.
His sad eyes look out the bus window.

His weathered hands and lined face
tell a story of the life he's had.

He smells of whiskey
and has a look of pain.

One morning his seat was empty.

Clock Man

I am the clock man.
I have a special place
for my second collection.

My room is full, floor to ceiling,
clocks telling different times.

Sometimes I listen to the different chimes;
sometimes I glance inside their little doors.

Each is set for a different place;
not one is right, not one is wrong.

I have no deadlines
in my tick-tock room.

Katie McDermott

To the Sea

The cold hits you
like a thousand knives;
it turns you numb.

Dark clouds dominate
over your head;
they do not harm you.

Slowly, you enter
a new world
where you swim.

Aisling McDonnell

Over Board

The sea was calling out to me
with its gentle swishing motions.

Dalkey Island juts above blue water
without a care, without a notion.

The sea calls again to me; I go.
A boat drifts past and seagulls fly.

Sinéad McGlacken Byrne

Waiting

By trying to change what
I cannot, I think with my head
not my heart. It is hard to block
emotions, I have had from the start.

It is she not me. You're mine.
I hate it being this way,
seeing you with her all the time
each and every single day.

Maybe it is not too late,
he might forget the past
and see what he has lost?
Perhaps this time it will last?

My Room

Why is the room so dark
yet outside is so bright?
I feel something is wrong
something, is not quite right.
I should be out in the sun
not stuck up here
doing my homework.

Sarah Murray

Posh and Becks

I love her; she loves clothes.
Am I in it for the publicity; who knows?
I hope our son will find his Juliet.

My match is on Saturday; must go place
a bet. Three-one to us; I'll get all the glory
and get the Sunday's front page story.

I live in a palace although I'm not a king
and my poor perfect wife really can't sing.

My hair has lots of different styles,
I change it everyday. So don't believe what
you read in the Star, I'm certainty not gay.

Persuasion

Let me please, just let me go.
I've already told you the answer is no.
So, there's no hope for me, not even a chance?
No, for God's sake it's an eighteens dance.
It's not a dance Mum; it's a club.
You think I'll let you sit in a pub?
It's not a pub...yes, there is a bar...
I suppose you'll want a lift in my car?
No, no it's fine I'll get a taxi.
You won't get in; you've no I.D.
Well, you know the form you signed?
It didn't say you were eighteen; I must be blind.
So, I can go is what you mean —
Well...no sex, no drugs and keep it clean.

Nicola Moran

In the Fields

Under the scorching sun
they work hard harvesting.

Everyone pitches and pulls
until all of the crop is uprooted

and the fields lie bare
for another year.

On the Face of It

There are many different kinds,
some circular, some square,
some with or without numbers
— clocks and watches.

Without them we would be lost
— perhaps with no time
we might find ourselves.

Sarah Meehan

Freedom

He sits there listening to the babbling brook
the sound causes him to stop and look.

Looking into the water he thinks of nothing
yet he is thinking of everything:

without structures, without boundaries or banks.

My Cupboard

Inside, cups sleep on saucers.
There's a tin with a biscuit or two
and in the corner a forgotten apple
hides, underneath the shelf with delft.

Aoife Naughton

Cameo

I remember the day we bought the land
my husband and I. We stood hand
in hand looking at our new life ahead.

A fresh start for me, and Ned,
many a happy memory we had.

Even though we struggled
when times were bad,

I look at it now and have no regrets
for this chapter of my life.

Aisling O'Brien

A Hairdresser's Dream

My life is a pair of scissors.
All day I stand, cut and snip.

I feel as if I have cut
half the world away.

Static

I cannot breath
through all this strife
and the coldness creeps
deep from within.

My mind is always
somewhere else,
somewhere better.

All around me
people change
and keep on going
but I, stay the same.

Emma O'Farrell

Sewing

I pick up
a small silver needle;
it gleams in the light.

I chose black thread,
stab my silver needle
into white cotton.

One by one tears
fall like a pattern
of sorrow.

Greener on the Other Side

The grass is overgrown
several feet high.
Thistles and nettles rule this field;
they are the ones who have most.

Half-way through the field
no murky browns exist,
only crisp greens with purple touches.

Aisling O'Rourke

The Guards

I sit at the window
behind a peeling frame.
The paint splattered steps
serve to increase my pain.

The nets look flimsy
yet it is my guard from life.
I sit just behind it,
it could be ripped with a knife.

If I escape
as I should try.
I will meet the next barrier
in a row of cacti.

View from the Charles Bridge

He looks out across the Vlatava
a piece of history ever flowing.

Nearby his dog is knee deep
in water, like a soldier of past times.

Now only the ducks are his enemies.
The bridge is majestic and grand.

Statues stand silently,
having weathered the storm.

Only the man will fall
as the statues live on.

Roisín O'Shea

Exploitation

I feel like I'm a hen picking up wheat;
my back is sore and so are my feet.

We have been picking up all day
in the scorching month of May.

People don't take much notice of us
as we carry their weight on our backs
for a penny a sack.

Waste

Looking out from where I stand
I see the beauty of the land.

The trees are wide awake and
green; the water is pure and clean.

The sky is blue like the sea.
When I look into it I see me.

I look behind, find my place
in this sea I can not face.

Tomoko Uchiyama

Real Dream

When I opened my eyes
I could see a strange view:
houses, walls, and
roofed domes
meeting the wet sky.

Everything is different
from my country
so I closed my eyes again.

A Different Sameness

As I learn about
the Celtic tradition
I think more of my own.

How we are losing
our culture,
throwing Japanese away
for the American way of life.

Anne Fitzgerald

Latitude

in memory of Sabrina Duffy

I have seen in your eyes an inner light
that takes me towards that place of longing.
Somewhere beyond the horizon I enquire
as to the precise co-ordinates of these sea
-grass fields where nymphs lull about in hulls:
mermaids comb their spirals beneath the sun.

In the same way you can quench the sun
from dog-days to leave an odd eclipse of light
trapped in starfish, guiding a forest of hulls
home to Atlantis; seahorses carry our longing
starboard, on course for deeper fathoms below sea
-level we speak in an Aristotelian tongue, enquire

without conch or a knowledge of Greek, enquire
as to whether angels come from the sun
of man made things or riddles by sea
-faring merchants, voyaging to new found light?
For Velasquez and the like stirred a longing
in wanderlust: men bend the ribs of hulls

a round the horn of capes, lost hulls
floored in myth, set oceanographers off to enquire
as to their whereabouts with sextant and longing.
Might dead-sea scrolls be read in the sun
or water cover the pattern of land in daylight
might Noah's Ark be hoisted to ride the sea?

If you raise the sash on weightless sea
-side towns: ice cream windows and upturned hulls
by a boatshed or hoofed moons cobbling twilight
strands, ebb and flow of equinox tides enquire
after white horses running a muck off sun
drenched hotspots, daiquiris by a pool stand longing.

And closing time brings no closure to this longing
save those who find their way below the silk of seas.
There monastral blues bath in a darker sun
fading deck chair stripes put out on other hulls
where divers find no shadows pass by or enquire
about the comings and goings of such light.

And in such light there rises a longing
for your sun-dark way with azure: sky to sea
edge-two-edge, little hulls push off to enquire.